From
HOSPITAL
to
HOSPICE

From HOSPITAL *to* HOSPICE

One Nurse's Journey Towards Grace at the Bedside

Susie Vincent BSN, RN, CHPN

WESTBOW
PRESS®
A DIVISION OF THOMAS NELSON
& ZONDERVAN

WestBow Press books may be ordered through booksellers or by contacting:

WestBow Press
A Division of Thomas Nelson & Zondervan
1663 Liberty Drive
Bloomington, IN 47403
www.westbowpress.com
1 (866) 928-1240

ISBN: 978-1-5127-1712-9 (sc)
ISBN: 978-1-5127-1708-2 (e)

Library of Congress Control Number: 2015917306

Print information available on the last page.

WestBow Press rev. date: 12/31/2015

Dedication

This book is dedicated first and foremost to my Lord and Savior, Jesus Christ. Without Him I would not be here to tell these stories, nor would I have been prepared for and continually blessed by this ministry of His.

To my husband Rob and children Katie and Ryan: Thank you for listening to me talk about the amazing moments that happen during a "normal" day of work for me. Thank you for your prayers, your support, and your encouragement not only as I entered the nursing profession but as I entered this holy ground of hospice work. I began my journey from "hospital to hospice" in early 2011 with a "calling." Patients and families also begin their hospice journey with a "calling," albeit of a different sort.

To my incredible patients, their families, colleagues, and the new friends God has brought alongside me on this journey: Thank you for affirming my mission when I told you I was called into nursing, then into hospice. This is a calling, and you understood. Fulfilling this calling is the only way hospice workers can truly survive the rough days, refill our spiritual reserves, and thrive in situations where the toughest people run out of a room. Only others that "do what we do" can truly understand.

If you have had the honor and privilege of caring for a loved one in hospice care, I pray that this book will give you strength and comfort. Thank you for allowing your hospice team to stand with you for a brief moment and may you use that experience to help others in their time of need.

Contents

Foreword

I have been a hospice nurse for over twenty years. Hospice nursing is a unique opportunity to come alongside patients and their families as they face a terminal illness. It is filled with a variety of challenges and rewards. It is important that the nurse and hospice team fulfill their duties with skill, sensitivity, and professionalism in order to make this journey easier to navigate. Those who have been successful have viewed their work as more of a calling than just another job for a nurse.

I have known a lot of nurses over the many years that have specialized in hospice that thought it would be easy nursing since they figured, "After all, the patients are dying." Nothing could be further from the truth since our patients are in multi-system failure. It requires a lot of skilled assessments, interventions, and heading up the multi-system interdisciplinary team to manage these patients' systems to keep them comfortable. It also requires dealing with the families and friends that are caring for these patients.

I remember meeting Susie Vincent when she came in for an interview. It was for an RN case manager position at the hospice I was working for at the time. I wondered if she would be joining us. I thought about what she might be asked in the interview. Hospice nursing is about the story of the patient's journey, but the nurse also has his or her own story as part of their history. I knew Susie would be asked to tell her story about what had drawn her to working with patients that are facing a life-threatening illness.

Susie was hired and has shown exemplary compassion and skill in caring for clients. She feels it is a call from God and that gives her strength to carry out her responsibilities.

I am honored to endorse Susie Vincent and her book. I found it hard to put down once I started reading it. She has captured the heart of nursing and shares some important practical insights that will help both nurses and patients to experience grace at the bedside as they prepare for their final journey.

—Debbie Summers BSN, RN

Preface

Like my patients, I too came to hospice from the hospital. Hospice patients have made a decision based on numerous factors. Maybe a treatment is no longer working. A cancer may have spread to the point that treatment will not be effective. They may still just be exhausted: tired of going back and forth between the hospital and home, tired of being poked and prodded, tired of fighting an inevitable outcome.

As soon as I began working as a hospice nurse, I knew without a doubt that I was born for this. I have felt compelled to write this book since, about things seen and unseen, and about the powerful moments I experienced almost immediately upon entering this field.

If you have a loved one who is seriously ill or possibly preparing to enter hospice care, first and foremost, please know you are not alone. This is not an easy time, but it can be a time of forgiveness, grace, compassion, and some very tender moments for all involved.

Our society does not provide sufficient education or information regarding hospice benefits under Medicaid, Medicare, or private insurance. Anyone who has faced a crisis can tell you how information presented during periods of calm is remembered better than information received during periods of crisis. Simply hearing the word "hospice" qualifies as a period of crisis for the families I see every day. Start asking questions now and become familiar with hospice care, as it is not meant just for the last few days of life.

Just as a woman's body knows how to prepare itself to deliver a baby, our bodies also know how to deliver us into eternity. If people spoke more openly about our mortality and felt comfortable enough to speak about death and the dying process, maybe this stage of life wouldn't be so taboo. As a result, families might be relieved that they have been prepared for the death of a loved one, and the process might be less frightening. I hope this book helps keep the conversation moving.

Hospice work is truly sacred ground. I pray you are blessed by this book and by the experiences contained herein.

Acknowledgment

I would like to acknowledge and thank the following people for giving me the words, courage, confidence, and editorial critique to proceed with this book: Jesus Christ, my husband Rob, daughter Katie (who also edited), son Ryan, friends Jeff and Peggy, text editor Sue, friends and co-workers Debbie and Jamie, nephew Bobby, niece Randi, and anyone else who has humored me by taking their time to read what is written here with the hope that it can help others in some small way.

Introduction

People often say to me, "I don't know how you do what you do."

Honestly, I don't know either! I depend on the Lord every minute of every day. Unbeknownst to me, He spent my whole life equipping me to be a hospice nurse! I pray for the right attitude and for gentle words that will comfort a family member. Many times, words have come out of my mouth that are not mine. How do I do what I do? I pray … a lot.

A 16th-century British evangelical preacher and martyr named John Bradford reportedly stated, "There but for the grace of God go I." I am well aware of what he meant by that. It could be me receiving information about end of my life, or that of a family member. In fact, it has been my family. We've gone down this road.

The collection of parallels from my own life contained in this book helps me to make sense of my experiences, my road to nursing, and the fulfillment of my life's purpose as a hospice nurse. In addition to the nudge I felt from the Lord, my sister's cancer diagnosis, palliative care, and dying process contributed significantly towards my leap of faith into hospice nursing. I honor her memory on each page.

Each chapter includes a flashback or remembrance of my family's journey during my sister Chris's life and struggles. I then correlate a story from my hospice nursing experience and discuss the lessons

I have learned through experiencing death both personally and professionally.

How do I do what I do? As you read, I believe you will see that each patient and family member I care for helps in some way to prepare me for the next. I am the one immensely blessed by the work I do, by my patients, their families and by our experiences together.

My hope is that, in some small way, you will find this little book a comfort to you and your loved ones. You may be either starting or finishing the same journey my family and patients have traveled. You may be caring for someone who is beginning the dying process. You may even be starting hospice care yourself. Regardless of the circumstances, you are not alone.

1

Always and Never

"I COULD NEVER DO HOSPICE," I SAID TO A FELLOW STUDENT AS WE
sat in our first nursing class together in 2005. She replied, "That's all
I want to do!"

You know what happens when you use words like "always" and
"never." God laughs and changes your plans and expectations. Little
did I know then, but hospice was what I was born for. It just took me
a little longer to get where God wanted me.

When I was five years old, all I wanted to be was a nurse. My
great-aunt Anna became a nurse during World War I. She was my
hero. She was the one who came and stayed with family members
when babies were born. She was the one who cared for and nurtured
each member of her family.

As an accounting student in community college (around 1982), I
remember a classmate saying she was going to "open the first hospice
in Eastern Oregon." I didn't know what hospice was then. I'm not sure
I had even heard the word "hospice."

During my junior year of college, while studying for a business
degree, I saw information about the nursing program and actually

thought "I could have been a nurse!" It was as if I had suddenly been reminded of the dream of my five-year-old self. When I received my Bachelor's degree in Industrial Management, I was envious of the nursing graduates.

Twenty years later, as I received my Bachelor's of Science in Nursing, I knew I was right where I was supposed to be. Usually I am a very tender-hearted person and cry easily during big moments. The day I graduated from nursing school I didn't shed one tear, I just experienced sheer joy.

I started as a floor nurse on a medical/surgical (med/surg) unit. I only agreed to do so because the Director of Women's Services told me I needed a year on med/surg in order to transfer to Labor & Delivery (L&D). I was *so sure* I was meant to deliver babies for a career! Little did I know, God had a different plan.

One year later, the L&D director moved to a different hospital. Things started changing for me very quickly. I changed to part-time status, which meant I floated a lot between different areas of the hospital. Very rarely did I work on my home floor of "med/surg." Next, my hands began losing strength and hurt all of the time. Surgery was eventually recommended due to the pain and weakness from osteoarthritis in both hands. There went my plan of delivering babies for a career. Then came The Diagnosis (Chapter 4).

It's ironic that I expected my nursing story to be about the *beginning* of life. God had a different plan and, to quote author Kathy Kalina, I became a "Midwife for Souls". My life's work was about to be dedicated to life at the other end of the spectrum.

2

Grace for Such a Time as This

I SHOULDN'T BE DOING THIS. I SHOULDN'T *HAVE* TO BE DOING THIS, I think to myself as I sit at the bedside of my dying sister.

My oldest sister, Chris, is dying at fifty-eight years old. She is only twelve years older than I am. Twelve years and immeasurable distances created by family dysfunction separate my sister and me. She is the oldest of five children; I am the youngest. We have two brothers and another sister between us.

Chris has at times fiercely loved me while at other times just as intensely despised me. She is a woman who had so much to teach, so much to give to others, and so much love to pass on. Her life *appears* to have been wasted—given over to resentment, to bitterness, to an inability to forgive, and to a gambling addiction.

She is still teaching, giving and loving as my sister's death plays a pivotal role in my becoming a hospice nurse. I just didn't know it at the time.

Every day, patients and family members receive news that instantly changes their lives. Sometimes that news begins a very long struggle, but sometimes the intense struggle is shortened by a quick death.

Like Chris, I have experienced a sudden, acute life-threatening episode. As a result of a ruptured ectopic pregnancy, I almost died in April 1991. Unlike my sister, I am still here. I don't know when my time will be up, but I know Who holds my time, my every and last breath. He has allowed me to stay on this earth for a little while longer, and I believe He has destined me for a specific purpose. Since my ectopic pregnancy, my husband Rob and I have been blessed with two wonderful children who are growing into incredible adults. My faith, like everyone else's, has been tested at times, yet here I am. That is grace!

God placed an immeasurable amount of grace before my family over a period of many years. In addition, He personally prepared my mother and each of my siblings to sit at Chris's bedside when her time came.

In October 1992, our daughter, Katie, was due any day. Our OB/GYN doctor found something he didn't like, and I was sent to a hospital that had a neonatal intensive care unit for testing regarding Katie's heart function. Her heart turned out to be fine, but then the doctors said her head was too small and that it hadn't fully developed. My husband and I were told she'd "most likely be retarded" (yes, that's the word that was used). The staff advised us to plan to deliver our daughter there and plan for her to be in the Neonatal Intensive Care Unit (NICU) after birth. Family members rushed to Seattle to be by our sides. The next morning a very healthy baby girl was born. Yes, she does have a "tic-tac © head" (to use her words), but it's an incredibly intelligent, packed-full-of-knowledge, beautiful head! Again, grace for such a time as this!

When my oldest brother visited my mom after her back surgery in the mid-1990s, he appeared as if he was going to bolt from the room, seemingly unable to handle all the tubes, lines, and machines attached to her. Fifteen years later, his son experienced major organ failure. My brother was a man who could barely stay in the room with my mom after her back surgery, but now he had to watch his own son go through a life-threatening crisis. Looking back, God was providing our family further preparation for The Diagnosis.

In 2007, my other brother was severely burned in a work-related accident and was transported to a hospital about three hours away from where he lived. Family members rushed to his side, taking my mom to be with her youngest son. My brother was in the Oregon Burn Unit for a month and has fully recovered. After all of this, our family has become very comfortable in hospital rooms around all sorts of equipment and procedures and we were prepared to sit at Chris' bedside.

⸺⸺⸺◦⸺⸺⸺

Grace is the only word I can use to describe what is needed, what is given, and what is received at times like these. We receive grace for acceptance, for strength, for forgiveness, and for moving past current struggle. According to oxforddictionaries.com (in Christian belief), grace is "the free and unmerited favor of God as manifested in the salvation of sinners and the bestowal of blessings".

Family and friends of hospice patients experience grace every day. Families come together, sometimes in reconciliation, sometimes in obligation. When a family member enters hospice care, there is a poignancy to the "H" word that opens wide the door for grace and love to come in.

One of the most beautiful things I experience in my work as a hospice nurse is the opportunity to see a patient as they are here and now. I don't see them as their family sees them. I don't see fifty years of family dynamics, as we call it: the wounds that have never truly healed, the unresolved individual and family choices that may have caused upheaval decades ago. I have my own set of luggage full of those items and I know what they're dealing with. I am able to encourage them and to let them know it is okay. Grace, and its unmerited blessings, help patients, families, and friends through times like these.

It is my prayer that as my own family members come to the end of their lives, there will be a compassionate, caring, objective observer to truly meet them where they are in that moment.

The end of life is a very sacred time, just as is birth. The dignity, respect, and love deserved by those at the end of life are of utmost importance. "Deserve" is not one of my favorite words and I use it sparingly. I think "deserve" implies an attitude of expectation and entitlement. However, on the flip side of "deserve" are grace and mercy. Grace and mercy show up hand-in-hand at the end of someone's life and everyone deserves both.

3

Hesitancy to Leave

My mom has a shoulder replaced in December 2006. She comes through surgery pretty well, until recovery. The phone call I expect from my sister comes later than I expect. When she does call me, she tells me Mom isn't ready yet to move to a regular room because she is having a hard time coming out of anesthesia. At the moment, my husband, my kids, and I are on the road, hurrying to get out of Colorado and en route to Oregon before a massive storm strands us somewhere between home and hometown.

As I sit at my mom's bedside, waiting for her to wake up, a young nurse and her supervisor come in to start an IV in the wee hours of the morning. I watch as my mom wakes and struggles to determine where she is. Fear is in her eyes and on her face, and it alarms me. Is it really so important that this young nurse needs to be "checked off" for IV skills at two o'clock in the morning on an elderly lady who is already scared and confused? Fellow nurses, please learn something from this. I didn't truly realize the potential impact on patients until I saw the heightened fear in my own mom's eyes when hearing words of

Susie Vincent BSN, RN, CHPN

instruction exchanged between nurse and supervisor in the darkness at 2 am.

The day after surgery, we learn why my mom struggled to come out of the anesthesia, why the doctor recommended rehabilitation for her at a nearby skilled nursing facility, and why she suddenly stopped smoking after decades. She had been diagnosed months earlier with emphysema, a form of chronic obstructive pulmonary disease (COPD). It all makes sense now.

Ten days later, my mom is in good shape. Her pain is under control and she hasn't developed any complications from the surgery. She participates in her physical therapy, performing her exercises as she should. She begrudgingly accepts the daily nebulizer treatments for her lungs and admits it helps her breathe. She ices her shoulder as she should every evening. I am ready to relinquish her care to my brother, but hesitant as well. I am in nursing school and have only one semester to go. I stay with Mom for almost two weeks post-surgery. After that, it seems to make sense for Chris to return from Alaska to help care for Mom in Oregon. Chris has been injured on the job and hasn't returned to work yet. She will be able to live with my mom to watch over and help her.

My family is ready to head back to Colorado. We load up the van and are ready to go. As we are pulling away from my mom's mobile home, my brother is on the porch smoking a cigarette. I wave "bye" to him and have an overwhelming feeling that this is the last time I will see him as he is now. I should yell "STOP THE CAR!" to my husband. I should get out and run to hug my brother. I should tell him I love him. I don't. I should have.

Less than two months later, he is in the Oregon Burn Unit at Emmanuel Hospital in Portland. He was life-flighted to Portland after being severely burned at work. My brother hates planes, especially tiny ones! He stays in the Burn Unit for about a month, and goes home with no further complications. I have not looked at him the same way since and should have heeded that little voice, that intuition to run and hug him, to tell him I love him.

—⊷·· —·✕❰◉❱✕·· —·✢⊶—

I have felt this same hesitancy to leave my patients since becoming a hospice nurse. At first I didn't recognize it for what it was: being in tune with my patient and knowing that something was changing. At the end of a visit, I might have already hugged them goodbye, held their hand or patted their shoulder as I headed for the door. When I found myself repeating those little actions, I began to recognize that hesitancy to leave. I knew they were getting close.

Sometimes the hesitancy manifests with the patient or family member holding my hand and not wanting to let *me* go. Sometimes they express it as "I don't know how to let go" or "I am getting close, aren't I?"

I was cautioned once not to "become another person to whom the patient has to say good-bye." That's all fine in theory, but once you have stepped inside their door, looked in their eyes, and held their hand, *it's too late.* Building that relationship with patients and families outweighs the inevitable difficult goodbye and sometimes I say goodbye more than once!

4

The Diagnosis

IT IS FEBRUARY 2010. I FEEL THE NEED TO SEE MY MOM. THIS DOESN'T happen very often. I am the daughter who finally realizes that the reason I send Mother's Day cards late every year is because I don't like shopping for them. The cards in stores just aren't right. They are too flowery and don't convey exactly what I would like to say, which is "Honor your father and your mother, that your days may be prolonged in the land which the LORD your God gives you." (Exodus 20:12, NASB). God has shown me time and again that this is what He expects of me, and I strive to do just that. The person I call my mom now isn't really the "mom" I had growing up.

Chris was really my mom from about age thirteen to eighteen. Chris, her husband of fewer than five years at the time, and their small son, Bobby, took me into their home when I was in the eighth grade. Their daughter, Randi, was born in the fall of my sophomore year of high school. Chris sought legal custody of me when she was just twenty-eight years old. I was twenty-eight years old when my first child was born. I can't imagine having an instant teenager! Chris and her family took me into their home because no one else wanted me, and the parent who did want me had a disease that made her want and *need* alcohol more.

⸺⸺⸺◆⸺⸺⸺

While visiting my mom, she is quiet, sad and nervous. Chris has just returned to Alaska. She has seen doctors, but hasn't received an official diagnosis yet.

My oldest brother calls me. Chris's diagnosis is Stage IV lung cancer that has already moved into her lymphatic system, colon, and liver. Chris tells him it is in the lymph nodes below the neck, but hasn't gone to the brain yet. She also tells him the doctors say it's a very, very aggressive cancer. I ask an experienced oncology nurse where lung cancers metastasize to, and she answers, "the brain." So it hasn't gone to the brain yet? I'm not buying it.

The doctors in Alaska give Chris two to four months to live with no treatment or up to twelve months with treatment. She is going to do chemotherapy once a week for three weeks, taking intermittent breaks, but the chemo is planned to go through July. She'll have a port surgically implanted in her chest, which will be usable for treatment after a month.

My oldest brother travels to Alaska to see Chris. His primary purpose is to determine where she stands spiritually. She assures him that she had accepted Jesus as her personal Savior during her teenage years. What a comfort that was, and remains to be.

In late summer 2010, Chris returns to Oregon from Alaska. Her children spend precious time with her. During this time, Chris's daughter, Randi, talks with my oldest brother about her mom's condition. Something's just not right. My brother, my nephew Bobby, and niece Randi take Chris to the emergency room in Walla Walla,

Washington. They need to know what is going on. She is now losing the use of her arm and leg on one side. Tests are run, and studies are done.

We find out that the cancer has, in fact, metastasized to Chris's brain. We find out that she has twenty-three tumors in her brain alone. Randi is a radiology technologist; she knows what this means. No wonder Chris is losing the use of her arm and leg.

By this time, I have been a Registered Nurse for three years. I can help. I am only working one night a week. I offer to come out and care for Chris at my brother's house. My offer is rejected. I make it again, but am rejected again. It's Chris's choice. I respect her wishes, pray for her comfort and peace, and wait patiently on God's timing.

5

Christmas Cookies

IT IS SEPTEMBER 2010 AND I AM BAKING CHRISTMAS COOKIES. I AM grateful that it's not a hot September day. My sister's favorite Christmas cookies are our family's sugar cookies, frosted by dunking them into a watery mix of hot water, melted butter, powdered sugar and vanilla. The consistency has to be just right, and of course there is no recipe! Since they are Christmas cookies, they need to be in the shapes of Santas, Christmas trees, stockings, hearts, with sprinkles and colored sugar on top!

While I am at it, I dig out a couple other favorite recipes and bake up a storm. Even though I was baking Christmas cookies in September, I felt like I was doing what I was supposed to do.

Is my sister ready to see me? I don't know, but the least I can do is make these cookies she loves and mail them to her. I know she will love and eat these.

She should be eating whatever she wants at this point. Those words come out of my mouth while talking to my brother. I am not sure I had ever said those words before, but looking back I can clearly see that they came from my heart, my hospice heart.

Instead of mailing the cookies, my kids and I spontaneously decide to take them to her personally over the upcoming Labor Day weekend. Chris starts crying as soon as she sees us. I walk over, bend down and hug her as best I can around her new accessory, a wheelchair. I tell her we brought Christmas cookies and ask if she wants some. Of course she does, and she doesn't want anyone else to have any the rest of the weekend because they are hers!

Sunday, September 5, 2010, is one of the sweetest days my siblings and I ever spend together. We spend hours together, all five of us. We just hang out with each other for the whole day. We share memories; Chris's mind is still very clear. She remembers things the rest of us can't. She ends up sharing her Christmas cookies with us, too. While we are there, she also enjoys all of the wonderful foods she loves, like peaches and cream, watermelon, and banana bread. What a gift, for her and us.

It doesn't matter if it's Christmas cookies in July or ice cream for breakfast. Patients should get to eat what is appetizing and comforting to them.

As a hospice nurse, I have often encouraged family members to allow the patient to eat whatever it is they want to eat, while they can eat it. Much of the time, especially early on, the family members feel that if their loved one will just eat something nutritious, everything will be okay.

I remind family members that family events like birthdays, parties, and holidays usually occur with everyone gathering in the kitchen. That's where wonderful memories are made, and those memories usually include food. We need to recognize that when a person is dying, they should eat whatever they want whenever they want it, as long as they can safely eat it.

One of my patients who had ALS (Lou Gehrig's disease) was losing her ability to swallow when I first became her nurse. As she progressed through her illness (she spent about four months on hospice), I encouraged her to make a list of those foods that she really wanted to eat before she could no longer swallow at all. We balanced those choices with the risk of choking and she was able to fulfill those desires.

6

911 – 9:11

OVER THE PAST SIX TO NINE MONTHS, EVERY TIME I LOOK AT A clock, a cell phone, the television, even the car radio, it seems like it is always the same numbers: 911.

What does it mean? What is going on? The obvious didn't seem to be what was in front of me at the time. I share this with a very dear Christian friend of mine from nursing school. We know something is up. It frightens, yet excites me, as I know God is preparing me for something, but what?

September 11, 2010, turns out to be a profound day for my dysfunctional family, as it's the day we think Chris may pass away. I have since learned that dates have significant meaning to hospice patients and families. Birthdays, wedding anniversaries, anniversaries of a loved one's death, are all important markers of time in their lives and continue to be important as a person approaches the end of their life.

The Palliative Care (PC) Nurse Practitioner caring for Chris calls Chris's kids and tells them they need to come see their mother. It's been a few days since the PC nurse has seen Chris, and the changes are drastic.

Randi calls me. By the time she calls, I am already researching airfare—without knowing the changes. How do I know ahead of time to start doing this? I believe it was the Holy Spirit preparing me for what was about to happen, and telling me to pay attention. I buy my ticket to fly to Spokane, Washington. From there I will drive to Walla Walla, a tiny town in Eastern Washington where Chris is hospitalized. Chris's son, Bobby, will fly to Pasco, Washington. Date of travel: 09/11/10.

3:38 a.m. A dream wakes me up. Not a dream really, but something I saw.

      I can only describe it like a hospital hallway, where a short, dark shadow dashes around a corner (oddly enough, a little like the old McDonald's Hamburglar©).

      It is brief, a vision I guess. I don't know what's going on, but I know enough to note the time because something has happened. I can feel it.

3:41 a.m. "R u up?" It's a text from Randi.

      Randi is in the hospital room with her mom, and has had to call respiratory therapy. Chris has taken a turn for the worse.

      "Can you call Bobby and see if he can get an earlier flight?" she asks me. I call him, but he can't.

Years and dysfunction and geography can separate, but never fully sever, relationships or connections. This sister of mine, who has alternately hated me and loved me, needs me now.

I arrive at the hospital at 1:00 p.m. My oldest brother asks me to call him when I see Chris to let him know whether he needs to come now.

At the hospital, Randi is alone with her mom. Chris is mostly out of it, her head lodged against the side rail of her hospital bed. Randi breaks into sobs when I hug her.

Randi tells me that during the night, she cried at her mom's bedside. Her mom told her, "Shhh." It's questionable whether she can see Randi or me. She can hear though, knows our voices and evidently doesn't want any sobbing!

Amazingly, Chris can still talk on the phone. She made her living on the phone and, since she lived in very small towns, the telephone was her lifeline. That makes sense. That whole day, the phone rings and her hand shoots up. She knows it's for her, and she's right. Why else would anyone be calling this hospital room?

"You need to come now," I tell my brother. We make plans for him to pick up Bobby at the Pasco airport and bring him to Walla Walla. He and Bobby arrive at the hospital around 4:30 p.m. All five of us siblings are there, one of us not for long—or so we think.

Chris is definitely seeing things we cannot. She focuses on a corner of the room. She smiles and points. Her face glows again. She reaches out toward the same corner. She is looking "through us." I am fascinated. What is she seeing?

In hospice, there is a term that gets our attention. A family member or caregiver will say "It's like (s)he is looking right through me!"

What we in this profession describe as "looking through" was given a fresh perspective from one of my sweetest patients ever. She was a devoted Christian and we connected instantly when I became her nurse.

As she lay almost unresponsive, in the transition phase of dying, I asked our team Licensed Practical Nurse (LPN) to visit this patient and see how she was doing. The patient's daughter was very nervous, unsure whether she could really provide the care her mom needed during this time. This visit today would be mostly reassuring the daughter as to her mother's comfort and that she was in fact providing exactly what her mother needed.

After seeing the patient, the LPN called me. "Susie, she's looking right through me," she told me. We both knew what that meant, and many tears were shed on both ends of that phone line.

The next week, the patient was still with us. I asked the same LPN to stop and check on her again. The LPN found the patient to be quite alert and awake. The LPN brought up the subject of "looking through her" with this sweet soul, and she responded, "Oh honey, I wasn't looking *through* you. I was looking *for* you *through all those people.*"

It's very rare that hospice workers get a chance to hear an eyewitness account describing what we've all thought was happening. What a blessing this patient was in such a moment of clarity. She was able to shed some light on these "things seen and unseen" happening in those moments.

7

Guardian Angel

DURING THE EVENING OF SEPTEMBER 11, AND WELL INTO THE NIGHT, it is standing room only in a tiny hospital room in Walla Walla, Washington. We tell stories, share memories, talk to Chris, and tease each other. When she says "stop," I tell her we are just teasing, and she says "stop" again. We stop. Memories and stories are important to share; evidently teasing is not!

We take turns helping her eat, take sips of fluids, keep her mouth moist, even rescue a peach pit from her teeth. She loves peaches even now! As I help her eat the peach, she grabs my finger, and we all giggle as she brings it ever closer to her mouth. I really think she is going to bite my finger off, but instead she tries to brush her teeth with it, which makes us giggle! Humor in the midst of pain is essential.

Chris asks multiple times whether I am there. I tell her I am here, and that all of us are here. I am glad it's important to her.

One of my brothers has a cell phone in his hand. He asks his big sister if she would like to talk to our dad. She hasn't talked to him but twice in the past twenty-five years. She holds her hand out for the phone.

What I witness is pure joy. She smiles during the entire conversation, and it is pretty much a one-sided conversation. My dad does most of the talking, because Chris isn't really able to talk at this point. Her face glows, her smile radiant. At the end, very clearly, we hear Chris say, "I love you, too." There is not a dry eye in the room.

After midnight, things begin to wind down in the hospital room. Bobby has his laptop with him and somehow is able to project pictures onto the wall. We look at pictures of his kids and other family photos. We order pizza (remember, memories are made around meals!).

It is late, but nobody wants to leave, especially one man. I refer to him as the "guardian angel." What's his name, with his wide shoulders and silver hair? He stood by the door with his arms crossed. He has been friends with Chris for more than twenty years. He just silently stands watch. That picture remains in my mind today. I think of Michael the Archangel, standing guard and continually protecting God's people, Israel (Daniel 12:1). Here was this smaller guardian angel, watching over my sister, holding a sacred vigil.

In fall 2011, I received a new admission to hospice, and he was an honest-to-goodness Guardian Angel. When I first met him I was a little afraid. He lived in a really rough area of town, with gang graffiti tagged on walls just up the block from his home. The first time I visited, I must have locked my car ten times before I reached the front door!

He was at least six feet, five inches tall, but the ravages of cancer were noticeable immediately. I sat across from him to start, unsure if he was ever going to let me touch him. I knew I had to approach him with nothing but respect and gentleness if I hoped to gain his trust.

There he was, sitting on a well worn couch with dogs and cats all around. Some of the animals I didn't even see until they were pointed out to me or they moved!

He allowed me to sit beside him to take his vital signs. The two dogs and two cats that were protecting this gentle giant were very territorial. Before long, one of the dogs was snuggled up in my lap, and I was "in like Flynn." Was I ever grateful to be a sucker for animals! When the dog trusted me, my patient followed suit. That same dog even tried a couple times to hitchhike a ride with me via my medical bag!

When he stood, he towered over me. I couldn't even imagine what he must have looked like when he was healthy. He had long, flowing gray hair and a beard. Now, he was skin and bones, frail and vulnerable, scared but not alone.

Admittedly, I live a pretty protected life out in the suburbs. I didn't feel comfortable in this space, but I also knew that Christ had intentionally put me here to care for this child of His. So I prayed unceasingly for comfort for the patient, for the patient to be able to trust me, for my safety, for darkness not to fall before I got out of there. They were all sorts of prayers, but mostly for him to pass peacefully.

By the time he died, I had handed his care over to another nurse on our team. That didn't stop me from rushing to his house to check on his wife and kids when I heard he had died. The tiny house was full, many people in shock or sobbing. When I got a chance to talk with his wife, we all cried openly. She knew he was no longer in pain, no longer suffering on this earth, and he no longer had a need for one of his Guardian Angel pins attached to his red beret. That tiny, delicate little pin represented to me what used to be a mountain of a man, and today that pin goes with me everywhere.

8

Are you going with me?

MY OLDEST BROTHER, MY NEPHEW BOBBY, AND I HEAD TO THE HOTEL to get some sleep. My other brother takes our mom back home. Time to rest and come back refreshed.

My other sister and Randi stay at the hospital that night. In the early morning hours, Chris wakes up, sits straight up and says "He cut in line!" Turns out there had been an unexpected male death across the hall that night. Chris tells Randi that she is "ready" and later plays "Eeny meeny miny mo," trying to select who would "go with" her. But then she tells Randi that she can't go with her, because Randi has kids.

A patient once asked me (on a Tuesday) if I was going to "go with" her. I said "No, I can't yet." By Friday, she was unresponsive. Pneumonia develops quickly in the compromised.

Each of us has given Chris permission to go—or so we thought.

Chris has an episode of what I now know to be terminal agitation. She is pulling at her chest port, pulling her gown off, etc. Later in the day, the nurses access her port and begin a morphine pump. It turns out that Chris actually requested a pump in prior discussions with her medical team for when the time came. Why didn't we know that before now?

The Palliative Care Nurse Practitioner that obtained the order for the pain pump approaches our family and asks if we would be interested in placing Chris in a different room. "It's not quite ready," she explains, but she thinks it will be much more comfortable than her current room.

She calls it a comfort room. It is a private room for the patient and has a glass sliding door that connects to a family room. This room has several chairs, a loveseat, a desk, a kitchenette, and its own bathroom. It's perfect. In this tiny little town in eastern Washington, my sister is going to be able to die with family and friends close around her. I am in awe of such a simple gesture that makes a huge difference. This hospital, Providence St. Mary's, and its Palliative Care program, have really seen and met a need not just for us, but for many others.

This family room is where the staff brings us comfort carts with coffee and cookies. It is where visitors can come and talk to us before they actually go in to see Chris. We can prepare them for what they will experience if they haven't seen her for awhile. It's where we can put our feet up, take a snooze, or just breathe.

My plane ticket back to Colorado was originally booked for September 14. When I try to check in online, my reservation cannot be found. I am too exhausted to spend a couple hours on the phone, so I book another ticket for the following day.

The past few days have been incredible. No matter how out of it

Chris seems, when the phone rings she continues to hold up her hand. She still knows it is for her and the rest of us ought not to get in the way of her phone calls! There comes a point where I joke, I am going to call her and say, "Chris, this is God. It is time."

What is she waiting for?

Before I leave, I am able to have some alone time with my sister. I hug her, I stroke her face, and tell her that I love her. She holds her hand to my face and wipes my tears.

I tell her it's okay to go. I tell her I am jealous. She is going to be with Jesus first! I tell her that her kids are going to be okay, that they have grown into such wonderful adults, and that we four remaining siblings will take care of them any way we can. I then return to Colorado.

The day we thought she would pass	September 11, 2010
I return home	September 15, 2010
Randi drives to Walla Walla one more time	September 16, 2010
Chris's friend from Alaska arrives	September 18, 2010
Chris's best friend from Alaska arrives	September 19, 2010
The day she actually died, around 3:00 in the morning	September 20, 2010

Randi has to return to central Oregon. Before leaving, she has a conversation with her uncle (over Chris's bed) and tells him that he needs to tell his sister that it is okay to go. That he will be okay. My big tough brother responds, "Why would I do that?" She needs to hear it to pass peacefully.

Randi calls me after she has left the hospital. She says she hopes it is the last time she is making that trip. It is close to midnight in Colorado. As she is driving, she says she sees a shooting star. "You better check on your mom," I tell her.

Chris's best friend from Alaska gets to the hospital late that night, spends some time with Chris, and then leaves to get some sleep.

3:20 a.m. September 20, 2010: I am awake before the phone rings. "She's gone," my other sister says. Somehow, I already knew. I call Bobby and Randi. They know, too, and they sound okay. Everyone has been called. One brother was by Chris's side. Had he finally told her it was okay to go? Or had she been waiting for her friend from Alaska? Likely both.

—————————————

I arrived at an assisted living facility around 4:00 p.m. for a first visit with a new patient's family. The patient was a transfer from a different hospice organization and the family had not felt supported or informed about what was going on with their mom. Sometimes a patient, their family, and hospice teams just aren't a good fit and things need to be switched out. Hospice workers need to remember that it's not about us, but about that patient and family. For whatever reason, this had not been a good fit.

Another team member, a social worker, met me there so we could do what's called a "co-visit." This co-visit tends to reduce stress on the family as they are introduced to a whole new team of faces, names, and roles. I often describe admission to hospice as being descended upon by a flock of birds.

The social worker and I had a few minutes to go in and see the patient before we sat down with the family. This patient had been up walking the halls just a few days prior. However, today, she was actively dying. She hadn't eaten for a couple of days, had lost the use of her legs, was unresponsive and displaying apnea (going several seconds without breathing). This family really needed information and direction immediately.

The social worker and I sat down with the patient's daughter and son, being as gentle as we could, and suggested they call whomever they thought might want to see their mom before she passed. The son was very upset with us, and I couldn't blame him. This was information they should have had before now. Signs that we could have prepared them for ahead of time included increased weakness, increased sleep, decreased appetite, and especially the apnea. She moved through the "transition" phase of dying very quickly and was now in the "active" phase.

The rest of the meeting went fine. Part of my discussion with families at this point has always been the need for them to give their loved one permission to go. Some people understand that, others don't (like my brother). For some reason, it is very important. When the loved one is a mom, I encourage all the kids to collectively give her permission to go, and then assure her that they will all take care of each other. The family in this situation didn't seem interested in that. When I left, they were assigning shifts for an all-night bedside vigil.

At 6:00 in the morning, they became weary and started discussing the idea of giving their mom permission to go. "Maybe we ought to do what the hospice nurse suggested and tell her it's okay to go."

They did, and their mom passed peacefully an hour and ten minutes later, much to their relief. They were almost lighthearted telling me about this when I stopped in around 7:30 a.m. to offer my condolences. They were on their way to grieving, and by having done this for their mom, in the long run they will realize they did it for themselves.

Do I know why this is so important? I do not. But it is.

Sometimes at the end of life, a person might be waiting for a certain date, a specific person to say one last goodbye, or for their children to leave the room. What has become apparent to me is that there are times the dying person is waiting for the hospice team to be in place so they know their loved ones will be comforted and supported through their grief.

9

Tiny Teacups

THIMBLES, REALLY.

I arrived at the patient's house a little earlier than I expected. The patient and chaplain were sitting together discussing our common Christian faith. I apologized for interrupting, but the patient didn't seem to mind. In fact, she seemed delighted that we were there together. She seemed determined for something, but I wasn't quite sure what for at that point.

This lady, who I watched become weaker and weaker each visit, unexpectedly exclaimed, "Let's have communion!" I wasn't sure we could have communion; the chaplain and I were on the clock after all. Could we drink wine? If she found some wine, we could only have just a little. She practically jumped up from her rocking chair, and headed towards the kitchen.

In the hall off the kitchen was a china cabinet, so we picked out little tiny teacups for her homemade cherry wine. We washed out the thimble-sized cups and went about the business of finding the old wine and something to use as bread for our informal, yet sincere and poignant, communion.

I turned my back on her for a moment, and found her bent over a cabinet trying to reach to the very back where an extremely dusty bottle of wine sat. I thought this dear, sweet woman was going to topple over onto her head fetching an old bottle of wine for communion. How in the world would the chaplain and I fill out that incident report?

With wine secured and bottle dust-free, she found a box of old, very stale Norwegian flat bread. The bread was about as dry as it could be without having been turned to dust!

Her blue eyes were twinkling, so excited for us to share in this moment of thankfulness. She was moving faster and easier than she had the past few months. Just incredible!

We all sat down, she in her little rocking chair, the chaplain and I on each side of her. The chaplain read the traditional "This is My body..." passages from the Bible (Mark 14:22). We shared communion as it was meant to be shared, as a remembrance among believers. We shared it simply, in complete acceptance and agreement as to what Christ had done for us on that cross in His perfect sacrifice of His body and His blood.

When I looked at her beautiful blue eyes again, they were teary but still dancing with excitement and love. You just never know when those moments are going to occur. I can't wait to embrace her in heaven and have communion again, this time in the literal presence of Christ!

People of the Christian faith tradition seem to cherish taking communion with their loved ones at the end of life. I know my sister did, as she shared communion with her children.

One of my patients, Jay, started his dying process almost immediately after taking communion with his longtime girlfriend. Taking communion wasn't that important to Jay, or so he said. It was important to his girlfriend.

Jay was a stubborn, difficult man to get along with, on the outside. On the inside he was pure mush.

The first time I met him, Jay was tooling around his skilled nursing facility in a wheelchair that he hated. It was uncomfortable. It was the wrong size. It was too heavy. The list went on and on.

One of the first things I noticed about Jay was that his chest seemed to be trembling all the time. Was he shaking from the exhaustion of trying to hold on to something?

As we got to know each other, and he accepted that I was doing my best to get him a more comfortable wheelchair, he began to trust me. When he told me that he had asked our chaplain to bring communion for him and his girlfriend, he invited me as well. "I would be honored, Jay," I told him, grateful for the invitation.

It took a week or so to arrange a day for communion, but it was beautiful. Jay was crying, his girlfriend was crying, and I was crying.

A couple of days later, Jay was actively dying. I couldn't believe it. I was sitting at his bedside, watching for what we call non-verbal signs of pain or agitation, and listening to him breathe. He was comfortable, but he was dying. The trembling in his chest was finally gone.

Looking back, I believe the trembling truly was exhaustion from trying to hold on—hold on for communion, hold on for his girlfriend and hold on, ultimately, for himself.

10

Do Not Rush into My Presence

My sister lingered for nine days past the day we thought she would die. That seems like a long time. It really isn't.

—————————

I have seen people die when I thought they'd be around for months. I have seen people stay in this life for weeks and months when I "just knew" they would die over the weekend. I have told people goodbye multiple times!

"Testing the waters," "dipping their toes in the water," "having a little rally," "their last hurrah;" these are all euphemisms for people who look like they are going to die soon but don't.

For a brief period of time, I wanted to know the timetable of when someone was going to pass. God showed me over and over again, that is not for me to know.

One of my patients whom I cared for fourteen months spent her last three months "testing the waters." I said goodbye to her, once again, this time on a Friday.

The following Monday morning I looked at her, bright eyes shining and smiling and asked, "Do you know the song 'Sittin' on the Dock of the Bay' by Otis Redding?" She said, "Yes, why?" I said, "Because you were there, with your feet in the water up to your ankles!" She and I had a good laugh about that. She knew she was close, but she also trusted the Lord to take her on His time, not hers, and definitely not on mine.

My patient with the tiny teacups spent weeks preparing to meet her Lord. She would have days of unresponsiveness, days when I could have cogent conversations with her, and days where I could watch her talk and animate with someone or something I couldn't see.

One day, I was sitting at her bedside and she wasn't talking to me. Her lips were moving, her eyes were fluttering back and forth, her hands and arms were moving purposefully. I pulled out a book she had given me months ago, a daily devotional called "Jesus Calling" by Sarah Young. This was an important book to this Godly woman, as she gave a copy to each member of her hospice team. I opened it up to read from that day's entry and shook my head at the faithfulness of God. It read, "Do not rush into My presence." I just smiled, finished the reading, quietly exited, and left her alone with her company.

11

Run, Ida, Run!

"I've had lung cancer before. This time it's back, and I'm not going to do anything about it. "I'm ready to go." Well, all-righty then!

"My mother-in-law died in your inpatient unit. That's what I want, too. It's a special place. I don't want to be in there that long, maybe a few days at most."

"Excuse me?" I asked.

"I want you to tell me when it's time to go into the inpatient unit, but not too early."

I told my patient, Ida, that I would do my best to honor our deal, but I also wanted to make sure she wouldn't be mad at me if I was off by a few days!

I was worried about her being mad at me, but I soon found out it was the other way around. She'd started smoking again. She would smoke in the other room, use a fan, use sprays, but I could always smell it.

"Ida, I don't care if you are smoking again," I assure her.

"You don't? I know I am not supposed to," she said.

"No, listen. If I did everything I was supposed to, I'd weigh a hundred and forty pounds. Clearly I don't!" We had a good laugh about that, and she understood I was not in a place to judge her or correct her in any way.

I learned so much from Ida, from her kids, and from how she lived her life. She had led a simple life of raising children and loving her "Handsome Jim" ("He was a Frogman, you know." These days we would call him a Navy Seal!). She was incredibly humble.

She gave me advice about how to raise children and how to avoid interfering when they became adults. She shared with me how to avoid money issues with kids. If one adult child needed financial assistance, the other child or children received a gift in the same amount.

She showed me the importance of wrapping things up before you die. She'd had her roof replaced due to a summer storm. It was now fall, very close to Thanksgiving. And she wanted to be sure she wrote the check to pay for her roof before she died.

In September, for some reason, she was really feeling the urge to drive her car again. Just a few blocks, she said. Her daughter wasn't with her this particular weekend, so Ida decided it was as good a time as any. She drove a few blocks to the Goodwill, and fell while standing in line. God bless the Good Samaritan who drove her home.

She called to tell me about it, and made me promise not to tell her daughter. "You have two days, Ida. You tell your daughter by then, or I will," I told her. When she did fess up, she called to report she had. I loved that lady!

It was a Saturday morning when her daughter called. Her daughter had moved in with her mom since receiving the news, and had cared for, shared with and walked through this with her mom. What a blessing that was for both mother and daughter. But this Saturday morning, Ida was in pain. She couldn't move very well.

She wasn't breathing very well. She was also spitting up more blood than usual.

I instructed Ida's daughter to call our triage nurse. I also called the triage nurse and asked her to begin Ida's transfer to the inpatient facility that day. As God planned it, my favorite hospice nurse (my mentor and trainer, Debbie) was on call that day and would be arranging Ida's transfer. I held up my end of our little deal, and so did Ida. She died a few nights later, taking advantage of a little span of time, literally minutes, where her daughters were not sitting vigil at her bedside.

In bed that night, I just tossed and turned. I knew she was close. It's common for me to wake up and just know that a patient has passed. This night, I just prayed and prayed as if I was talking to Ida. In this type of prayer that I have never prayed before or since, I finished by silently yelling, "Run, Ida, Run!"

Her daughters believe she needed that little extra nudge to run towards Jesus and leave her children behind.

12

A Little Dignity Please

IN HOSPICE WORK, WE TALK A LOT ABOUT PATIENT DIGNITY. AT THE end of life, there are things you say and things you don't. These guidelines extend to the elderly, the ill, and to those who might not be terminally ill but require assistance in their daily lives. For example:

Briefs. Call them briefs. Or call them Depends©, if they're Depends©. Or tab-top briefs. Just do not call them diapers.

Diapers are for children before they are potty-trained. They are not for aging adults. Even some Electronic Medical Records systems refer to them as diapers, which infuriates me.

Things you say or do:	Things you don't say or do:
"Let's get you clean and dry."	"Let's change your diaper."
"I am going to turn on the light."	Just flip on the lights without warning.

"We're going to change your linen."	Roll the patient side to side without telling them.
"We're going to reposition you."	Move them without telling them.
"My name is Susie, and this is…."	Talk over them, or about them.

When you are going to turn them to their side, tell them.

When you enter the room, put your hand on their forearm to let them know you are there, and that you need to turn on a couple of lights. "I'll do my best to not disturb your comfort," I tell them.

I have had the responsibility of caring for "comfort care only" patients in the hospital, and I talk to them just like I talk to anyone else. This comes as a surprise to some staff members, and I encourage them to consider that the dying person can still hear, and so requires comfort and reassurances along the way.

Dying patients hold onto their hearing the longest. Let's remember that and give them dignity by our words and our actions. They deserve that.

13

Any Other Way?

SEVERAL TIMES A YEAR, A NEWS STORY CATCHES MY EYE ABOUT HOW a long-married husband and wife die within hours or days of each other. I have often considered how much of a role sheer "human will" plays in the dying process. These stories seem to reinforce my ponderings, but more importantly they remind us of just how strong love can be.

In hospice, we look at the patient and family as one unit, as one patient.

Sometimes a hospice nurse will end up with a patient and spouse as two patients, at the same time.

She was a feisty little thing, diagnosed with end stage COPD. Just her breathing consumed every calorie she took in. She was comfortable on her medications, so that was a blessing.

Her husband used to sit on their couch, right beside her, and nearly demand that I give "a good report." He was a sweetheart. He loved her so much.

All of a sudden, my sweet little lady started getting very emotional, started reminiscing about some of the times in her life she felt were the most important. Something was up.

I couldn't figure out what was going on. Until one day, I was on the phone, on hold with her doctor and I was looking at her field chart in my hands. Her patient sticker caught my eye. She had been a hospice patient for six months!

Six months is a milestone to a hospice patient, since your doctor has to certify that (s)he thinks you have a life expectancy of six months or less in order to admit into hospice care. Clearly, this cutie pie had gone past her six months.

We processed that a little bit, talked about it, laughed about it, and then things changed. She was declining. She always insisted on sleeping in her room, up a flight of six or seven stairs, where she and her husband had slept so many years together. He insisted as well. Her husband had recently had a few falls, and now a major stroke over the weekend. He became my patient as well.

One of the saddest things I have ever seen was a marriage bed, over sixty years in the making, removed from their bedroom and replaced with side-by-side hospital beds. I couldn't breathe when I first saw that. Their daughter was distraught. Her dad was close to dying. She was looking to me for comfort and direction.

I remembered something he had said months ago, about being in the armed services, and not being very proud of something he had done. He seemed to be in a bit of terminal agitation, and I asked his daughter if she would pray. She said he had been very worried about not being saved. So I suggested the Sinner's Prayer. She nodded. I said to him, "I know you can hear us. I know you can't speak. But you can repeat in your heart what is being said if that's what you feel you need to do." His daughter couldn't lead in prayer due to her tears and sobbing. I started with the Lord's Prayer as He taught us to pray in Matthew 6:9-13 and then followed with a Sinner's Prayer. Romans 10:9-10 tells us "that if you confess with your mouth Jesus as Lord, and believe in your heart that God raised Him from the dead, you will be saved." His daughter and I said "Amen," tears freely falling onto his hospital bed linens. He became more calm and comfortable immediately after that.

He died two days later.

His wife, my original patient, lasted another couple of months. She rallied a little bit after his death, but then began her final decline.

Their daughter was left to grieve both of her parents in such a short amount of time. She took a great deal of comfort in the fact that they went so closely together, and said they wouldn't have wanted it any other way.

14

On Guard

Before I became a hospice nurse, I had heard the stories and read the books about the incredible interactions that happen between pets and their humans during the end of life. Some cats could predict which patient would be the next to die in a skilled nursing facility. Those accounts always fascinated me. Now I wish I had made a copy of every single one of them to read and re-read on an ongoing basis.

When I was a young girl, one of my brothers lost a thumb in a work-related accident. Our family dog, an Irish Setter named Murphy, was really not our family's dog, but my brother's dog. He was kind of a hyper, excitable dog, but he was a sweetheart when he stood still, usually only for seconds at a time.

When my brother lost his thumb, he was in the local hospital for a few days, and both boy and dog missed each other terribly. Everyone thought it would be a great idea for the dog to go see his boy. That was a big mistake!

My brother's hand was wrapped up like a boxing glove, and when the dog came close all he did was growl and look like he was ready to attack. My brother was crushed! I include this as a reminder that even though our pets become part of our families, caution is always advised as it's hard to predict how they will react in different situations. I am sure Murphy's reaction had to do with the smells of the hospital on my brother, his robe, and his wheelchair. Whatever it was, the dog wanted no part of it. I wasn't very old, as my brother is ten years older than me, but I will never forget that encounter.

When Chris was dying, we learned there was a comfort dog available to visit. My sister was not the biggest dog lover in the family, at least overtly. She would tease the rest of us about how we spoiled our dogs, and then we would catch her secretly feeding one of them ice cream from a spoon!

The comfort dog did visit, but it seemed to be more for my mom at that point, which was just fine. This was a much better interaction than my brother had had as this comfort dog was trained to be in tune with what was going on.

I believe animals know and sense what is happening and can help if we let them. We need to respect their place in that situation. In hospice, they do have a place and it is right alongside their human.

I tell my patients and families to pay attention to the pets. They know things before we do. I don't know if it is chemical smells or physical reactions they pick up on, but they know.

"Susie, he won't let the dog up on the bed with her. He needs to be up there! Do something!" The private caregiver was at her wit's end with this situation.

Wait a minute. This dog had been getting up and down on this bed for over four years. Why would the patient's spouse not allow the dog up now? Something's up.

The patient had been experiencing increased pain the past few days. Doses had been increased, changes made to the pain medication regimen. When the patient complained of pain, the husband felt it was because the dog was up on the bed and was causing the increased pain.

Not so. This was a change of condition for this patient. I talked to the husband and reassured him that the dog was not causing this pain. I even asked the patient, in front of the husband, if she wanted the dog on the bed beside her. Of course she did!

The husband relinquished, and the dog took his rightful place next to his mom.

A few weeks later, all of a sudden this dog would not get up on the bed. He laid under the bed, he jumped in my lap, he took refuge under a chair next to the bed. But he wouldn't get up on the bed. Something's up.

The patient had experienced another change of condition. I have learned to watch these animals because they are trying to tell me something through their actions.

A male patient had a cat that just loved him. Cats usually don't come across as overly affectionate, but this one did. Whenever the patient's heart rate was elevated, we'd call the cat. After about three to five minutes of stroking this beautiful black cat's fur, the patient's heart rate would be decreased by about ten percent. Amazing. When the patient died, this loyal feline took his rightful place up on the bed next to his dad.

The little lady in an earlier chapter who asked me if I was "going with" her had a couple of cats in her home. I had been visiting her for at least six months, when I had to graduate her (she was doing so well she was no longer appropriate as a hospice patient) for being so stable, and then re-admit her when she quickly lost a bunch of weight.

About a week before she asked me if I was going with her, one of the two house cats came and positioned him/herself right smack between us. That had never happened before. The cats usually were very stand-offish and would eye me from a distance. But not this time, not this cat.

This big orange cat was letting me know something's up. I told the patient's daughter what had happened, and to be watching for a change. Sure enough, a change of condition came in the form of pneumonia.

Watch the animals. Watch for changes in their behaviors, and in their usual routines. If the animal is usually clingy but starts to withdraw, pay attention (and vice versa). Even if you have known the animal all its life, never assume they are going to be the same at the end of their human's life. Caution visitors to approach them carefully. Approach the patient slowly, not over-enthusiastically, until you have a chance to see what the animal will do.

Allow them to be on the bed. Allow them to be present when and after their human is passing. They already know, and they need to grieve, too.

15

The Hardest Conversation

I SIT, WATCHING MY MOM AS SHE SITS BESIDE HER DYING DAUGHTER. I have no idea what thoughts, if any, are running through her mind at the time. But she sits, talking very lovingly and soothingly to my sister. She holds Chris's hand, alternating between holding and stroking it.

We've had a good conversation with the Palliative Care Nurse Practitioner regarding exactly what is happening, that Chris is moving very quickly toward the end of her life. We discuss that her comfort is the ultimate goal and that she won't be awake much from here on out, that food and fluids are unnecessary at this point unless she asks for them. My mom seems to understand what is being said and seems at peace.

Chris is moved over to the comfort room, so the hospital staff brings us a comfort cart filled with coffee, juice, and cookies. We start to settle in, greeting visitors, taking turns going down to the cafeteria for a real meal, or just to take a break and get a little air.

All of a sudden, my mom asks, "Should we be feeding Chris or something? She'll never get better if she can't eat!"

I thought we just covered this subject; evidently not. My mom had listened, but didn't *hear* what was being said.

· · —·§· · · —· · ·>·(·)·◄·· ►— · · ·ჳ·◄— -

I see this every day in hospice. Providing education about what the body does and doesn't need at the end of life sometimes has to be done multiple times. The family needs to truly understand what is going on. It's hard to absorb and accept difficult information during a time of crisis and upheaval.

Loved ones are concerned about the patient starving to death. They might understand that a human body can go without food for awhile, but not water. At times they seem accepting that natural dehydration at the end of life is actually a good, natural, endorphin-releasing process. They "get" that the body knows how to shut itself down, just like a woman's body knows what to do when a baby is being birthed.

When you think about it, a lot of favorite memories revolve around family get-togethers and holidays. When friends and family spend time together, they usually gather in the kitchen or dining room. In the kitchen, traditional favorites are slaved over and prepared without ceasing for upcoming Thanksgiving and Christmas celebrations. There's a reason loved ones want to feed their dying family member. It's what we do. It's how we nurture. It's hard to let go.

· · —·§· · · —· · ·>·(·)·◄·· ►— · · ·ჳ·◄— -

"Susie, I just don't think I can do that to him," his wife blurted out when I arrived.

This was not a routine visit today, just a supply drop. Or so I thought.

The patient had indicated to me a week prior that he didn't want his artificial nutrition continued. He had a feeding (PEG) tube, which had recently needed replacing. He had been admitted to hospice care after a midnight trip to the emergency room. I was hoping that with the replacement of the PEG tube, he wouldn't have to suffer yet another trip to somewhere he didn't want to go. He had lost the ability to walk, to sit upright, to talk, to swallow safely, but his mind was intact. He could communicate by pointing, blinking his eyes, his facial expressions, and with his hands.

His wife had not been present during my visit last week, and that was a good thing. That meant she was able to take a little break for herself and visit with her children. Now, I really wished she had been there. A private caregiver was in the home but not in the room while I was there.

The patient and I had a very good conversation with me asking questions, and he answered by holding up his fingers (one for yes, two for no).

As always, we started with pain? No pain.

Are you having difficulty breathing? No.

Were you able to sleep last night? Yes.

Does it hurt or burn when you urinate? No.

Did your wife give you the artificial nutrition last night? Yes. But he also grimaced.

Does that make you physically uncomfortable when she hooks up the tube feed? Yes.

Is it too much volume of fluid? Yes.

Do you want to decrease it? Yes.

Do you want to stop it? Yes. Definitively Yes. One finger held up with a determined look in his eyes. Wow. Now what?

Do you want to talk with your wife about what you've just requested? Yes.

I knew that at least one of their children had tried to talk to Mom about stopping the tube feeding. That adult child had tried to point out that Dad would not want these to continue. He was tired, he was suffering. He had very deep pressure wounds on his body. He was skin and bones. How long would this go on?

I told my patient that I understood his request and that at our visit early next week we would have the same conversation with his wife by his side. I had a responsibility to him to communicate that to his wife.

We had already started pre-bereavement work with this family, but I knew I had to call our Bereavement Counselor and the other team members prior to having this conversation (Chaplain, Medical Social Worker, and Certified Nurse's Aides) so they would know what was happening ahead of time and be sensitive to the subject at their next visits.

We had that conversation and I did my best to make it as close to the original as possible. It didn't go very well. His wife was in shock. Dumbfounded, she really didn't react at all. I saw anger in her eyes, as well as fear. At the same time, I saw relief in my patient's eyes, along with great love and concern for his wife. When I left the house that day, I called the Bereavement Counselor and asked her to see this family as soon as possible.

The next day, I needed to drop off some supplies I'd ordered for his wounds. The wife met me at the door, said, "Susie, I just don't think I can do that to him," and immediately started sobbing, collapsing into my hug.

I held her for as long as she needed, and prayed for the right words to comfort this beautiful soul. This loving wife, who treasured her husband, who wasn't sure she could face life without him. This wife, herself a nurse, wanted to heal him, to cure him, to "fix" him. But this patient's ultimate healing was not to occur on this earth, in this life.

"He is not asking you to do this **to** him, he is trusting you to do this *for* him."

Thank you, Lord. That was exactly what she needed to hear. She looked at me, still crying, but hearing my intention which was, after all these married years, who else could he trust more fully to honor his wishes?

From then on, she had a resolve about her that never wavered. He stayed with us for a few more weeks. I'm not sure how, but he did (again, that sheer human will).

Two days before he died, we had a similar conversation about his nebulizer treatments. This man hated those nebulizers. She knew his lungs were compromised and she had been giving him treatments three to four times a day. We looked over all the medications she still wanted to continue, she would say the name of the medication and look at me. If it was a comfort medication, I would nod and say, "Yes, continue that." But if the medication was unnecessary, I would shake my head, "No," and she would reluctantly cross it off his list that she kept track of so diligently.

He died peacefully in his home, in his bed, and surrounded by his family, including his dog. He was comfortable, he knew he was loved tremendously, and his wishes were honored.

As hard as it was to have that conversation, with his wife watching as he held up one finger to indicate he wanted to stop being fed, she heard him. She really heard him.

Afterword and Onward

Thank you for taking your money and your time to purchase and read this collection of accounts from my own life, my sister's life, and the lives of the patients I have been privileged to care for during this most sacred time.

When I began my career as a hospice nurse, it was such a perfect fit! It was like God took all these different pieces of me that He created and snapped them into place like the last piece of a jigsaw puzzle. It's what He made me for, what I was born for.

He has laid it on mine and my husband's hearts to open a hospice house for folks that are truly at the end of life, some of them having no one to be with them and no resources to pay for other care. The proceeds from this book will be used to establish and maintain Christ's House Hospice, a not-for-profit home where the dying will be cared for, comforted and comfortable in their last days, and treated with the dignity they so deserve.

Thank you.

The following pages are intentionally left blank in order for you to record your own thoughts, prayers and experiences that you will want to remember.

Printed in the United States
By Bookmasters